WORD GAMES

BY MARI BOLTE

Norwood House Press

For information regarding Norwood House Press, please visit our website at www.norwoodhousepress.com or call 866-565-2900.

Credits
Editor: Heather DiLorenzo Williams
Designer: Sara Radka
Fact Checkers: Ann Schwab, Lauren Hapgood, and Reyzl Grace MoChridhe

Photo Credits
Cover: ©Mitch Hutchinson / Shutterstock; page 3: ©San Francisco Chronicle/Hearst Newspapers via Getty Images / Contributor / Getty Images; page 4: ©Serhii Khanas / Shutterstock; page 5: ©FP Creative Stock / Shutterstock; page 7: ©Creative Stock Creations / Shutterstock; page 9: ©MirageC / Getty Images; page 13: ©solidcolours / Getty Images; page 15: ©Jose Luis Pelaez Inc / Getty Images; page 16: ©MediaNews Group/Boston Herald via Getty Images / Contributor / Getty Images; page 19: ©Brian Cahn / ZUMAPRESS / Newscom; page 20: ©NurPhoto / Contributor / Getty Images; page 23: ©Chad Robertson Media / Shutterstock; page 25: ©FP Creative Stock / Shutterstock; page 26: ©Tada Images / Shutterstock; page 29: ©Doug Benc / Staff / Getty Images; page 30: ©Frederick M. Brown / Stringer / Getty Images; page 32: ©Chepko Danil Vitalevich / Shutterstock; page 33: ©Tada Images / Shutterstock; page 35: ©Gina Hsu / Shutterstock; page 36: ©Brian Cahn/ZUMAPRESS / Newscom; page 37: ©martinova4 / Shutterstock; page 39: ©Lisa Maree Williams / Stringer / Getty Images; page 40: ©Ponomarenko Anastasia / Shutterstock; page 42: ©David Becker / Stringer / Getty Images; page 43: ©Brandon Bell / Staff / Getty Images

Library of Congress Cataloging-in-Publication Data
Names: Bolte, Mari, author.
Title: Word games / by Mari Bolte.
Description: North Mankato, Minnesota : Norwood House Press, [2023] |
  Series: A great game! | Includes bibliographical references and index. |
  Audience: Ages 8-11 | Audience: Grades 4-6 | Summary: "An introductory
  look at word games. Describes the history of the games, introduces
  creators and innovators, highlights competitions, and provides insight
  about the games' future. Informational text for readers who are new to
  word games, or are interested in learning more. Includes a glossary,
  index, and bibliography for further reading"-- Provided by publisher.
Identifiers: LCCN 2022042016 (print) | LCCN 2022042017 (ebook) | ISBN
  9781684507399 (hardcover) | ISBN 9781684048472 (epub)
Subjects: LCSH: Word games--Juvenile literature.
Classification: LCC GV1507.W8 B56 2023 (print) | LCC GV1507.W8 (ebook) |
  DDC 793.734--dc23/eng/20220916
LC record available at https://lccn.loc.gov/2022042016
LC ebook record available at https://lccn.loc.gov/2022042017

Hardcover ISBN: 978-1-68450-739-9

Scrabble™ is a registered trademark of Mattel, Inc.
WORDLE™ is a registered trademark of the New York Times.
Wheel of Fortune™ is a registered trademark of Califon Productions, Inc.
Scripps National Spelling Bee™ is a registered trademark of The E.W. Scripps Company.
Words With Friends™ is a registered trademark of Zynga, Inc.
This book is not associated with Scrabble, Wordle, Wheel of Fortune, the Scripps National Spelling Bee, Words With Friends, or any of their associated partners.

©2023 by Norwood House Press. All rights reserved.
No part of this book may be reproduced without written permission from the publisher.

359N—012023
Manufactured in the United States of America in North Mankato, Minnesota.

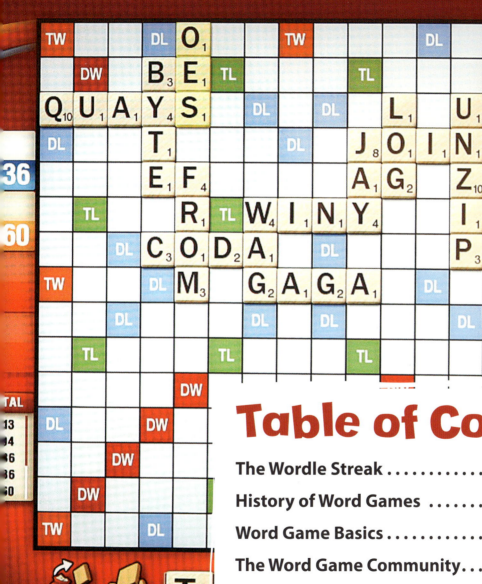

Table of Contents

The Wordle Streak 4
History of Word Games 6
Word Game Basics 14
The Word Game Community 24
The Future of Word Games 34

Glossary 44
For More Information 45
Index 46

The Wordle Streak

It's time to solve the daily **puzzle**. You stare at your computer screen. Thirty white squares stare back at you. A keyboard of gray squares waits below. You take a deep breath. Then, you make your first guess.

As you try to guess the word of the day, the white squares turn gray, yellow, or green. A yellow square lets you know that you picked the right letter but it's in the wrong spot. Green means that letter is in the right spot. But gray means you're wrong.

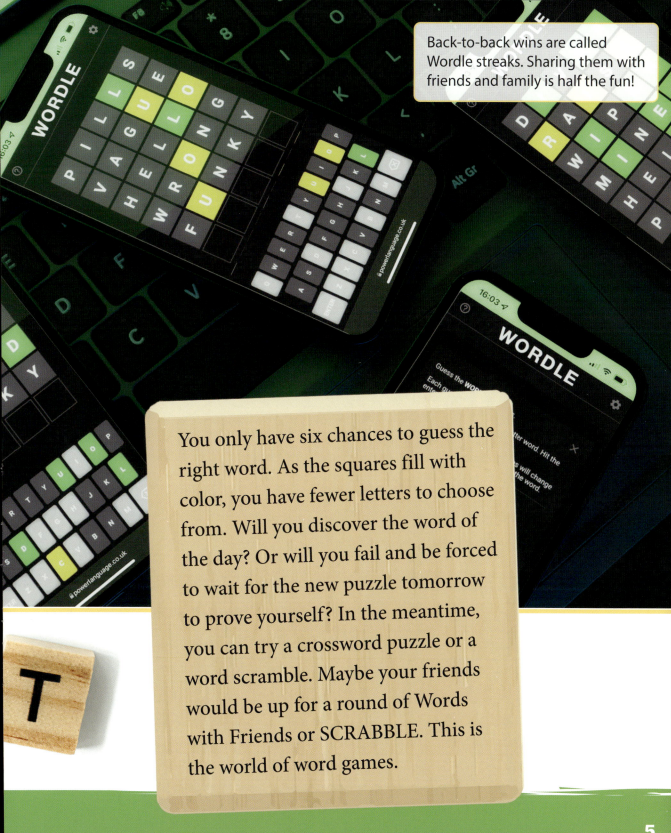

Back-to-back wins are called Wordle streaks. Sharing them with friends and family is half the fun!

You only have six chances to guess the right word. As the squares fill with color, you have fewer letters to choose from. Will you discover the word of the day? Or will you fail and be forced to wait for the new puzzle tomorrow to prove yourself? In the meantime, you can try a crossword puzzle or a word scramble. Maybe your friends would be up for a round of Words with Friends or SCRABBLE. This is the world of word games.

History of Word Games

People have enjoyed word games since the time of the ancient Romans. One of the oldest word puzzles is called word squares. This puzzle has letters that make the same words that can be read both across and down. The first known version is called the Sator Square. It has been found in **ruins** dating back to the 1st century CE. It reads:

S A T O R

A R E P O

T E N E T

O P E R A

R O T A S

Since then, people have searched for words on the back of cereal boxes or on restaurant menus. They unscramble letters to spell real words. And they make guesses to fill in blank spaces.

DID YOU KNOW?

Sudoku is also a magic square puzzle. It flexes your brain in the same way. It is traditionally played with numbers instead of letters. But there are other ways to play too. Colors, shapes, or even images and symbols can be used. There is also a word version of Sudoku! It is called Wordoku.

S A T O R
A R E P O
T E N E T
O P E R A
R O T A S

When translated, the Sator Square reads, *"The farmer Arepo works a plow."*

Sator Square grew into new games. The letters of the square hide another puzzle. They can be rearranged in a cross shape to spell PATER NOSTER going both up and down and sideways. Later, Sator Squares were used as a way to ward off bad luck. People believed evil could not stay in the same room as a Sator Square.

People challenged themselves to come up with their own version of Sator Squares and word scrambles. During England's Victorian era (1820–1914), parlor games became popular. These were group games that were played indoors.

Fictionary was a guessing game. One person looked for the strangest word they could find in a dictionary. The players wrote down what they thought the word meant. Then, they read their ideas aloud and chose the one they thought was the best.

Queen Victoria herself took part in word games. She is credited with creating the "Windsor **Enigma**." It was published in 1861. This puzzle is called a double acrostic. It's a poem. The first letter of each line spells out a word when read from top to bottom. The last letter of each line does the same.

DID YOU KNOW?

Riddles were another kind of puzzle game popular during the Victorian era. Riddles are questions or statements. They have **puns** or double meanings as their answers. The first known riddle is around 4,000 years old.

Pater Noster means "Our Father." The leftover *As* and *Os* had religious meanings.

History of Word Games: Time Line

1st Century CE
The first Sator Squares are created.

1913
The first crossword puzzle with a pre-drawn grid is published in the *New York World*.

1931
The game Lexiko is invented; by 1948, it has been renamed SCRABBLE and has a game board and new rules.

1950
The *New York Times* begins printing a crossword puzzle every day.

1968
The first word search is published.

2019
Wheel of Fortune celebrates its 37th season and tapes its 7,000th episode.

2021
Josh Wardle makes a guessing game. He calls it Wordle.

Lewis Carroll, the author of *Alice in Wonderland*, made a game called Doublets. He published it in 1879. Players started with two words of the same length. Players were challenged to turn the first word into the second by changing one letter at a time to make new words. For example, the solution for *head* and *tail* would be:

HEAD   HEAL   TEAL   TELL   TALL   TAIL

Crosswords did not look like they do today. Players only got the clues. **Grids** were much more simple. They had to make sure the lines **intersected**. On December 21, 1913, the *New York World* newspaper found themselves with space to fill. Journalist Arthur Wynne created a diamond-shaped grid. He called his puzzle Word-Cross. There were 31 clues. The idea was instantly popular.

The *New York Times* Crossword

At first, the *New York Times* thought that crosswords were just a fad. In 1924, they published an opinion column that predicted the game would disappear quickly. But during World War II (1939–1945), they saw that people needed a distraction. Finally, on February 15, 1942, the *Times* became the last major daily newspaper to publish a crossword. Every Sunday, they released a challenging crossword puzzle. By 1950, there was a new puzzle every day. There have only been four *Times* crossword editors since that first crossword in 1942. They are Margaret Farrar, Will Weng, Eugene Maleska, and Will Shortz.

The first word search in America was published in 1968. People liked how simple they were. Players did not have to be able to read well. They didn't have to solve clues or be good at math. They just had to match letters. Teachers started using them in classrooms. Restaurants put them on their children's menus.

In 1931, a game called Lexiko Words was invented by a man named Alfred M. Butts. Players chose letter tiles and used them to make words on a grid. By 1948, it was known by a new name. SCRABBLE became one of the best-selling games in America. By 1954, more than 4.5 million copies had been sold. The first SCRABBLE tournament was held in 1973.

In 1973, a show called *Shopper's Bazaar* played on NBC. The "shoppers" spun a wheel. Then, they picked letters to fill in blanks in a puzzle. Eventually, the show was renamed *Wheel of Fortune*. The 2,400-pound (1,089-kilogram) wheel is instantly recognizable around the world.

Word games reached a new high in 2021. A software engineer named Josh Wardle had an idea. He made a guessing game for his partner, Palak Shah. Shah loved word games. The game's name was a play on his last name, "Wardle." Wordle was an overnight success. Today, millions of people play every day.

Word searches help people get comfortable with new words.

The Scripps National Spelling Bee

Spelling bees challenge competitors to outspell the competition. Each person is asked to spell a word aloud. A mistake eliminates them from the competition. The words get harder as the number of people decreases. In 1925, the first Scripps National Spelling Bee was held. American newspapers could **sponsor** students to work toward competing at the national level. More than 2 million children entered. Nine finalists went on to compete in Washington, D.C. The winner was 11-year-old Frank Neuhauser. His final word was *gladiolus*. Today, more than 555,000 people tune in to watch the Bee live on TV every year.

Word Game Basics

There are many different types of word games. With their black-and-white blocks, crossword puzzles are instantly recognizable. They usually share similar rules. The number of blocks is the same on every side. If the grid is flipped upside down, it will still look the same. All the words are at least three letters long. And the white squares, where the letters are written, are connected.

Word searches are another common game. Players are given a list of words to look for. The words are hidden in a grid of letters. They are usually hidden forward, backward, up, and down. Sometimes, they can be found diagonally. The words will always be in a straight line.

> ## DID YOU KNOW?
> Crossword puzzles are usually 15 squares tall and 15 squares wide. However, the *New York Times* Sunday crossword is 21-by-21.

Crossword puzzles come in a variety of difficulty levels.

Each country's National SCRABBLE Championship pits the top players against each other. The winner will go on to compete at the world level.

SCRABBLE is a board game. It is sold in more than 120 countries. Kids participate in Youth SCRABBLE programs throughout the US.

Players draw seven letter tiles from a pool of 100. The first player makes a word with their tiles on the game board. Letters must be across or down. No diagonal words are allowed.

Each letter is worth between 0 and 10 points. Special squares on the game board add bonuses, like double word or letter scores. The player adds up the points from their word. Then, they draw enough new tiles to have seven again.

The next player must make a new word with their letters. However, their word must use one of the letters already on the board. The game continues until all letters have been drawn and one player runs out of tiles.

High Scores

There are a few ways to get ahead in SCRABBLE. A player who uses all their tiles in one play gets a bonus of 50 points. Setting letters on bonus squares can boost a score too. The word *MUZJIKS* is worth 29 points, but when played as a first word, it is worth 128 points. Setting letters on top of bonus squares drives up the score even more. In 2006, player Michael Cresta played *QUIXOTRY* in a tournament. He earned 365 points. His final score was a record-setting 830 points. In 2012, Toh Weibin beat the world record with a tournament score of 850.

Wordle challenges players to uncover a randomly selected five-letter word in six tries or less. Letters can be used more than once in a single word, but the word is never **plural**. With each guess, players receive hints about their choices. If a guessed letter is not in the final word, it turns gray. If it is in the final word, but not in the right place, it turns yellow. If the letter is correct, and in the right place, it turns green. A keyboard underneath the Wordle block also shows which letters have been used and which are correct.

Wordle experts can make the game harder with a visit to their game settings. Hard Mode only shows correct letters when they're in the right place. There are no yellow hint boxes.

A new puzzle comes out every 24 hours. Everyone in the world has the same word. This lets friends compare notes. They can brag about fast guesses. Wordle also keeps track of a player's progress if they play on the same device every day. It shows how many games have been played. Their win percentage is recorded. A player's current and overall win streaks are also stored. And a graph shows how many guesses a player has taken to solve the puzzle over time.

DID YOU KNOW?

The *New York Times* bought Wordle in 2022 for more than $1 million. The *Times* offers other word games. Their crossword puzzle is famous. Another *Times* game, Spelling Bee, challenges people to spell words using just seven letters.

Josh Wardle liked the idea of daily crosswords. He intentionally designed Wordle to follow the same once-a-day format.

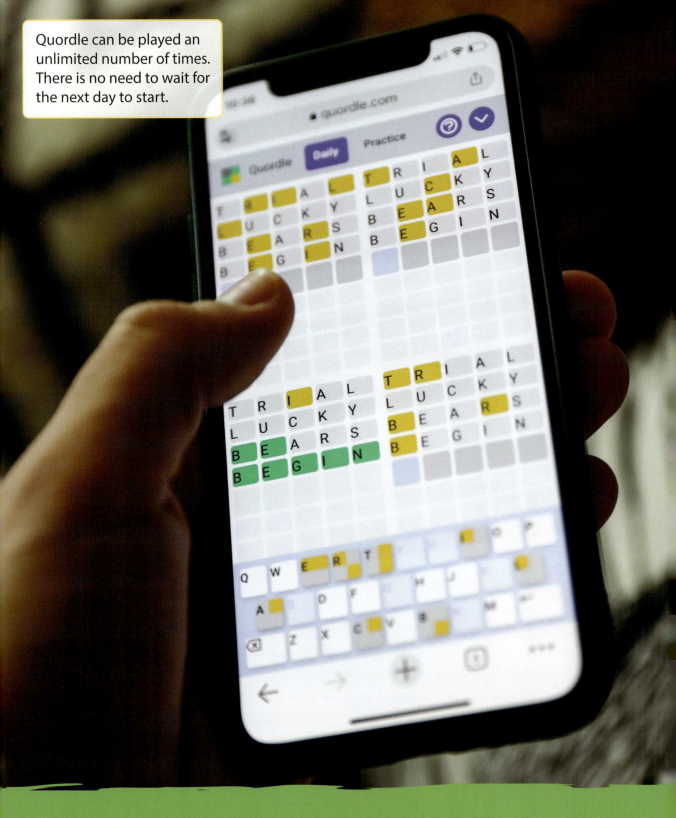

Quordle can be played an unlimited number of times. There is no need to wait for the next day to start.

The popularity of Wordle has led to many spin-offs. Quordle challenges players to solve four Wordles at once. But they only get nine chances to guess all four words. Each Quordle word gets its own 6-by-9 block. Each guess fills the same line in each block. But the colored hints are different in every block, because each word is different. Guessing words with a lot of vowels or common words can help one become a Quordle master.

Worldle takes players around the world. The game shows a shaded outline of a country. The country must be guessed in six tries. Instead of letters, though, the gray, yellow, and green squares tell players how far away—in miles or kilometers—their guess is. The more green squares, the closer the guesses are geographically.

Crosswordle combines Sudoku with Wordle. A 20-square grid must be filled with the correct letters. The bottom row starts out as a whole word with all green letters. Other rows have yellow or green blanks already filled in. Players use these hints to figure out the five other words.

DID YOU KNOW?

There were originally 12,000 potential five-letter Wordle answers. Wardle and Shah cut the list down to around 2,500 words.

Heardle tests music fans. The first second of a popular song is played. The players have six shots to guess the song's title and artist. Once they've found the right song, they can enjoy the entire track.

Nerdle is a number version of Wordle. It is eight blocks wide by six blocks high. Players guess a mathematical equation. Instead of letters, they use numbers and basic symbols. Each answer must contain an =. An example might be 20 + 10 = 30. A number must go to the right of the = sign. Standard **order of operations** is followed. That means * and / come before + and –.

Redactle is for those who like an added challenge. Players are given a Wikipedia article. Every word, except basic words such as *in, is, of, or* and *is* are **redacted**, or blanked out. Users try to fill in those blanks. They have unlimited tries, but the number of guesses and matches are recorded. There are hundreds of blanks and 10,000 possible articles. Players learn about a new topic as they play.

The Odds Are in Your Favor

Some people like to think of a different word to start each game of Wordle. Others use the same word every time and go from there. But some words make it more likely that you'll be able to uncover the answer faster. *Wheel of Fortune* players often choose the letters *RSTLN* to help them solve puzzles. That's because those letters are found in many common words. *Slice, tried, close*, and *trace* are useful starter Wordle words.

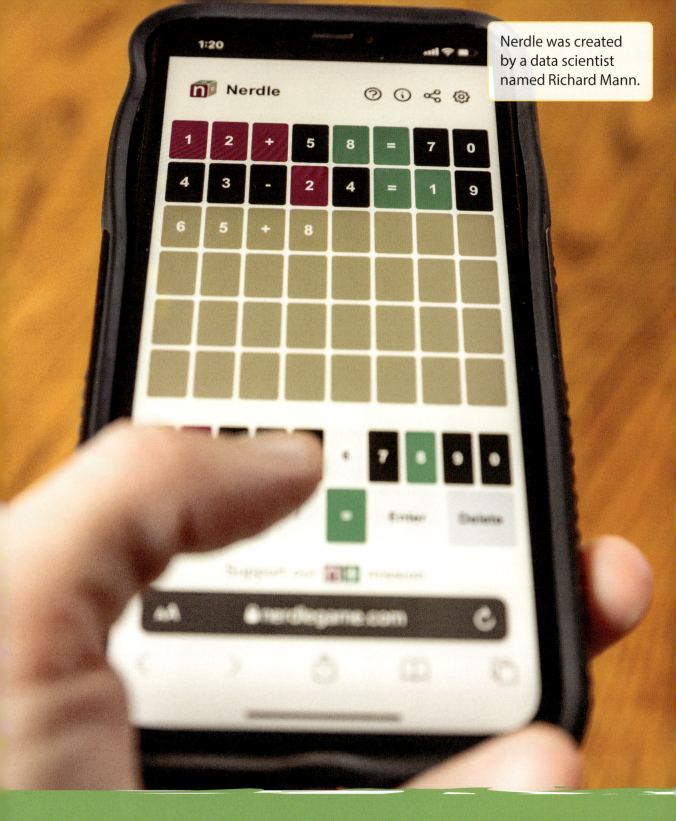

Nerdle was created by a data scientist named Richard Mann.

The Word Game Community

When Josh Wardle made Wordle in 2021, it was just for him and his partner. Then, their families joined in. They liked it enough that Wardle released it to the public in October. On November 1, there were 90 players. Two months later, 300,000 were playing. By January 2022, there were 2 million people waiting for the newest puzzle every day. People used #dailyWordleClub to compare answers on Twitter.

Playing word games is something people can do on their own. But they can also play with friends! Wordle is meant for sharing. The puzzle is the same for everyone no matter where you live. Comparing results is half the fun.

DID YOU KNOW?

Companies began using Wordle's format to advertise on social media. The gray, green, and yellow squares encouraged people to order chicken wings or vote in local elections. Companies with board-shaped logos, like LEGO and Triscuit, made Wordle boards to look like bricks or crackers. Google even asked, "What's a 6-letter word for a thing that will help you solve 5-letter words?" (Spoiler alert: the answer was "Google!")

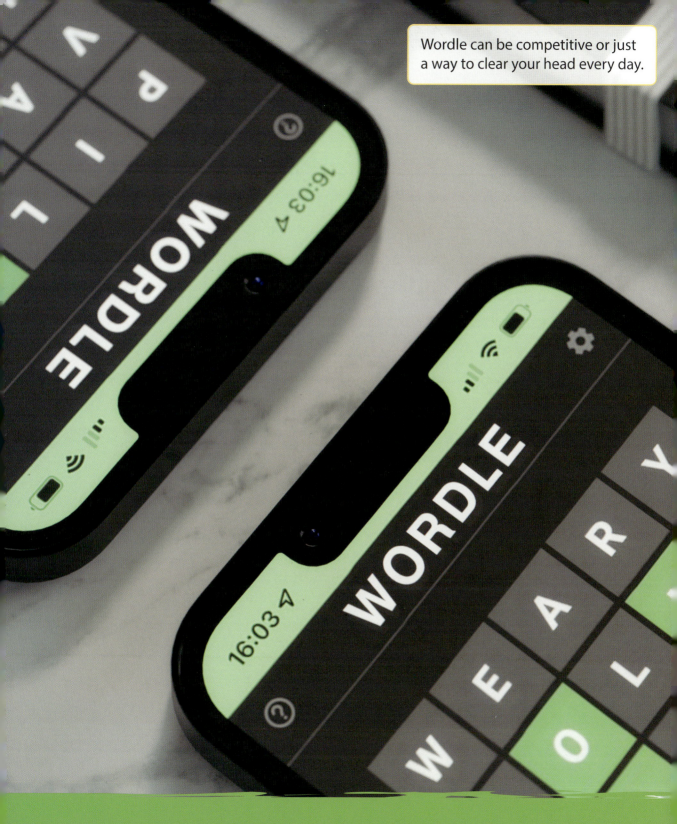

Wordle can be competitive or just a way to clear your head every day.

Some people were upset when Wordle moved to the *New York Times*—their stats did not carry over. However, guides on how to restore Wordle streaks were quickly shared.

It's easy to share Wordle results on social media. Players can brag about guessing on the first or second try. Or they can complain to friends about just missing out on the right word.

The share button helped spread the word about the game. People saw their friends' Wordle posts. They tried the game out for themselves. Soon, Wordle was **trending**. Between January 1 and January 31, 2022, Wordle was mentioned 8.2 million times on Twitter. That's pretty impressive for a game that doesn't have an app and isn't on social media itself.

Wordle isn't the only way to play word games with friends, though. Words With Friends is a SCRABBLE-like app. It came out in 2009. Players can challenge their friends with the touch of a button. More than 10 million people use it every month.

SCRABBLE has an older and even more competitive edge. There are official, in-person tournaments with real cash prizes. There are strict rules all players must follow. The players are serious about the game. During the Scrabble Players Championship, hundreds of people compete in 31 rounds over a five-day period.

DID YOU KNOW?

Words With Friends was the developers' second app. Chess With Friends was released eight months earlier. Both games' popularity was thanks to their ability to connect people over the internet.

Wheel of Fortune is probably the most famous and best-paying word game. It is one of the longest-running game shows in America. More than eight million people tune in every night to watch the wheel spin. They guess the answer along with the TV. Hosts Pat Sajak and Vanna White have worked together on the show since 1982.

Three contestants play against each other at once. Each spins a wheel when it's their turn. The wheel stops on a prize, or a number value. That number is how much a correct letter is worth. Say the wheel stops on $200. The person who spun picks the letter T. The puzzle has three Ts in it. So the contestant has won $600. If there are no Ts, the contestant makes no money. They lose their turn. Then, the next player gets their chance to play. If they think they can solve the final puzzle, they shout it out.

Celebrity Wheel of Fortune pits famous people against one another. They can play for prizes as big as $1 million. Their winnings go to charities of their choice.

DID YOU KNOW?

Michelle Loewenstein became the first *Wheel of Fortune* contestant to win $1 million. She finished her turn on the show with a total of $1,026,080. The record stood until 2013, when Autumn Ernhard left with $1,030,340. Sarah Manchester was the third, and most recent, winner. In 2014, she won a total of $1,017,490.

NFL players participated in *Celebrity Wheel of Fortune* in 2005.

Tyler Hinman (left), pictured with Will Shortz, has won the American Crossword Puzzle Tournament seven times.

Some people solve puzzles professionally. The American Crossword Puzzle Tournament is the nation's oldest and largest competition. It celebrated its 45th year in 2023.

The current *New York Times* crossword editor Will Shortz founded the tournament in 1978. The Stamford Marriott in Connecticut noticed business was slow in the winter. They talked to Shortz. He had just moved to the area. They asked him to come up with an idea. During the first year, 149 contestants showed up. Today, the entire hotel can be reserved on the weekend of the competition.

People can compete in five different divisions. There are also special prizes for certain age groups. Throughout the weekend, there are seven puzzles to solve. There is an extra one for the final championship. Everyone gets the same puzzle. Speed and accuracy are rewarded. Incorrect letters mean points are lost.

Solve From the Couch

Crossword Tournament From Your Couch was the largest crossword tournament ever. It took place over a week starting on March 20, 2020. The online competition drew in 1,815 puzzle solvers from around the world. Nearly 1,275 of those competitors were participating in their first crossword event. It was live-streamed and synchronous, which meant people solved the puzzles at the same time, no matter where they were. Tournament puzzles can be downloaded and solved by anyone interested.

Not all word games are played online or as part of a game show or competition. There are plenty of ways to enjoy an afternoon with friends and family for fun.

Bananagrams is similar to SCRABBLE. Both games use word tiles. Players pick a certain number of face-down tiles to start with. These face-down tiles are the "bunch." Everyone flips over their tiles at the same time. They spell out words and place them in an intersecting word grid. The grid can change as much as it needs to.

The first person to use all their letters yells, "Peel!" Everyone grabs another tile from the bunch. Eventually, there will be fewer tiles left in the bunch than there are players. When that happens, the first person to use all their letters and call out "Bananas!" is the winner.

Boggle is a letter and dice game. Sixteen dice have different letters on each side. Shake the dice, and then set them in a 4-by-4 grid box. Players have three minutes to think up as many words from those letters as they can.

DID YOU KNOW?

Word games are great activities for casual players and fierce competitors. There are even websites that can help you make your own word searches, puzzles, or Wordles.

Abraham Nathanson thought SCRABBLE was too slow. He wanted to make "a game so fast, it'll drive you bananas." Bananagrams was born.

The Future of Word Games

In February 2022, the *New York Times* added Wordle to its Games app. They already published the *New York Times* Crossword, the Mini Crossword, Spelling Bee, Tiles, Sudoku, Vertex, and Letter Boxed. In June, the game moved to the newspaper's website. The purchase brought tens of millions of new users to the *Times*.

The game has also brought word games into people's homes. Millions of Tweets about Wordle have been seen. During its most popular time in January 2022, there were 500,000 new Tweets about the game every day.

There's a Bot for That

In April 2022, the *New York Times* released WordleBot. The tool lets players check their results and rate their skills. It rates the player's skill, luck, and steps. Both skill and luck rate players on a scale of 0 to 99. Skill measures how the player was able to minimize attempts. Luck shows if their guesses reduced the number of possible solutions. Steps counts how many overall tries were used. WordleBot ratings can be shared online.

The *New York Times* saw nearly 390,000 new digital subscribers after it bought Wordle.

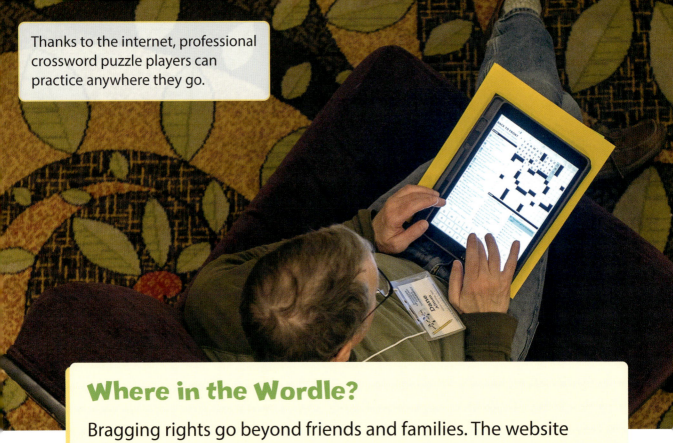

Thanks to the internet, professional crossword puzzle players can practice anywhere they go.

Where in the Wordle?

Bragging rights go beyond friends and families. The website WordTips analyzed Twitter data to see where and how people were playing. Although the Wordle is always in English, the United States is only ranked #18 in the world. But some locations are holding up the rest. North Dakota holds the highest national average in the world, with a score of 3.65. St. Paul, Minnesota, is the fastest American city, with 3.51 tries per game.

Sweden is home to the best overseas players in the world. Swedes guess the right answer after an average of 3.72 tries. But Canberra, Australia, is the fastest global city outside the United States, with 3.58 tries.

Players who want a more competitive game can join the Wordle Cup. The website hosts multiplayer tournaments. People can join public rooms. There, they can compete with people around the world. A scoreboard keeps track of the fastest times. Private rooms can be created for harder puzzles. Games can also be played all day.

In 2021, the American Crossword Puzzle Tournament did something new. They hosted the first-ever live Wordle competition. Contestants used a smartphone app designed by Josh Wardle. It was made just for the tournament. Hundreds of people competed in six rounds. Sid Sivakumar, a 25-year-old crossword constructor, was the winner.

Wordle Wars are another way to compete. Colleges around the country host Wordle tournaments to bring students together. In-person and virtual events help students meet new people who share their interest in word games.

DID YOU KNOW?
Word games help people connect. They can play with family members or friends who are far away. Even those with little in common can enjoy word games together.

Some word gamers have their eye on a bigger puzzle. The Scrabble Players Championship began in 1978. It has been held every one to three years.

Gamers must play in tournaments to receive a rating. That rating decides which of four divisions they are placed in. The first-place winner in the highest division wins $10,000.

The World English Language SCRABBLE Players Association hosts tournaments for top players. In 2019, New Zealand-Malaysian player Nigel Richards won for the sixth time. Richards is good with words. In 2015, he won the French-language SCRABBLE world championship. He doesn't speak any French. It took him nine weeks to memorize a French SCRABBLE dictionary.

Mistaken Identity

Josh Wardle's game is web-based. It has never been available in app form. But in 2017, 18-year-old Steven Cravotta built a game app for fun. He named it Wordle! They could pay to unlock more levels. Cravotta quickly forgot about it. But in January 2022, he noticed that his app had been downloaded 200,000 times in just a week. Cravotta reached out to Wardle. Together, the creators decided to donate the money made from Cravotta's game to a **nonprofit organization** that mentored young people.

Alex Lam participated in the 2021 National SCRABBLE Championships in Australia.

Twitch has any game anyone could ever want to watch.

Video game players love word games too! Wordle-type games challenge users to guess words from their favorite video games. The app Twordle is a version of Wordle. It is paired with Twitch, a video **streaming** platform. Viewers can work together to solve the puzzle. They use the chat feature to talk to each other.

Some have wondered if Wordle could enter the competitive world of **E-Sports**. WeWordle pits two players against each other. But there's also a timer. The players take turns trying to guess the word. Each turn lasts 15 seconds. And there's no once-per-day limit. Rematches can be instant.

Squabble invites even more players to the game. Squabble Blitz can be between two and five players. Squabble Royale can handle six to 99 puzzle solvers. Like Wordle, there's one word and six tries. But wrong guesses take away health points (HP). If you run out of HP, the game is over. Correct guesses earn back some HP and also damage opponents. Replay mode lets winners relive their victories and gloat about great guesses.

DID YOU KNOW?

Competitive E-Sports are a $1.4 billion industry. Gamers can compete in tournaments to win big prizes. The highest-paid gamer in the world is Jonathan "NOtail" Sundstein. He has won nearly $7 million by playing the game Dota 2.

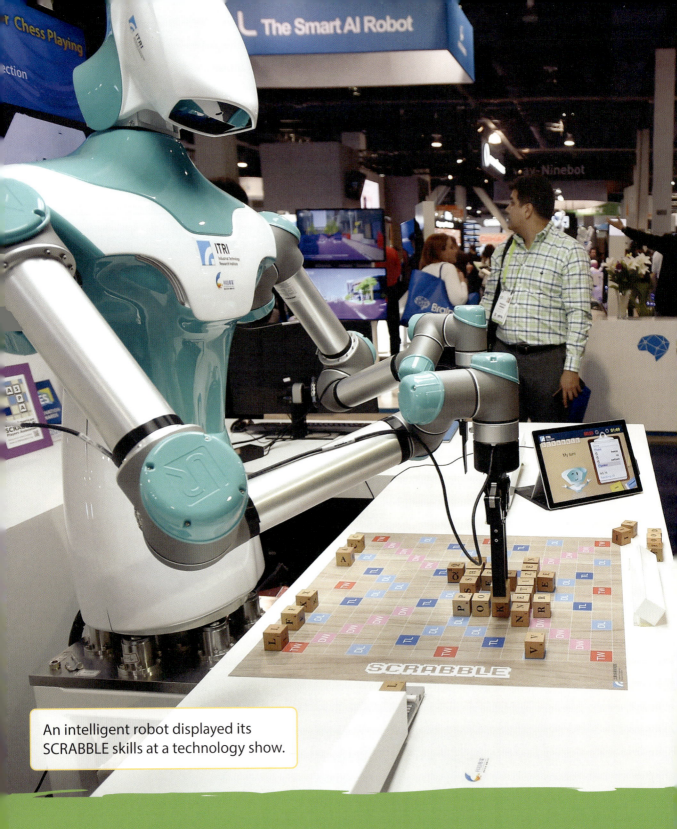

An intelligent robot displayed its SCRABBLE skills at a technology show.

Word games have kept minds busy for hundreds of years. Whether it's a simple word search, a complex crossword puzzle, or a Wordle match between friends, people love circling, unscrambling, and typing letters. There's always a new puzzle to solve or even a new game to create. Some play them to stretch their minds. Others want to relax. Still others have a competitive itch that needs to be scratched.

The next great word game is out there, just waiting to be discovered. Until that time, players will be waiting with their pencils sharpened and their touchscreens at the ready.

DID YOU KNOW?

In January 2022, college student Owen Yin leaked a full answer list for the Wordle puzzles through October 2027. Each answer is stored within the Wordle website's code. Players could download a script that would locate that day's answer.

Glossary

enigma: something that is mysterious, puzzling, or difficult to understand

E-Sports: multiplayer video games played competitively in front of an audience

grids: networks of lines that cross each other to form a series of squares or rectangles

intersected: two or more things that passed or are laid across each other

nonprofit organization: a group with the goal to benefit people, rather than making money

order of operations: set rules that state the order in which multiple operations should be solved

plural: more than one

puns: jokes that play with different possible meanings of words

puzzle: a game, toy, or problem designed to test the mind

redacted: edited or censored

ruins: the remains of a building

sponsor: to provide money or equipment to a person or an event

streaming: sending content over a computer network to be viewed by others

trending: currently popular or discussed online

For More Information

Books

Goldfield, Anna. *The Mind-Blowing World of Extraordinary Competitions: Meet the Incredible People Who Will Compete at ANYTHING.* New York, NY: Neon Squid, 2023.

Polinsky, Paige V. *Board Games.* Minneapolis, MN: Bellwether Media, Inc., 2023.

Websites

Crosswords for Kids (https://www.crosswords-for-kids.com/) A collection of kid-friendly crossword puzzles.

Discovery Education: Puzzlemaker (https://puzzlemaker.discoveryeducation.com/) Make, print, and share your own word puzzles.

Wordle (https://www.nytimes.com/games/wordle/index.html) The official Wordle site.

Index

American Crossword Puzzle Tournament, 31, 37

Bananagrams, 32

Boggle, 32

Carroll, Lewis, 11

Cravotta, Steven, 38

Crossword Tournament From Your Couch, 31

E-Sports, 41

Fictionary, 8

Lexiko, 10, 12

New York Times, **The,** 10–11, 14, 18, 31, 34

New York World, **The,** 10–11

Sator Square, 6, 8, 10

SCRABBLE, 5, 10, 12, 17, 27, 32, 38

Scrabble Players Championship, 27, 38

Scripps National Spelling Bee, 13

Shortz, Will, 11, 31

Sudoku, 6, 21, 34

Twitch, 41

Wardle, Josh, 10, 12, 21, 24, 37–38

Wheel of Fortune, 10, 12, 22, 28

Windsor Enigma, 8

Wordle, 4–5, 10, 12, 18, 21–22, 24, 27, 32, 34, 36–38, 41, 43

Wordle Cup, 37

Wordoku, 6

Words With Friends, 5, 27

Wynne, Arthur, 11

About the Author

Mari Bolte has worked in publishing as a writer and editor for more than 15 years. She has written dozens of books about things like science and craft projects, historical figures and events, and pop culture. She lives in Minnesota.